FAMILIES

Explore family concepts in a caring classroom.

by
Sherry Burrell

Art by
Catherine Minor

FIRST TEACHER PRESS
First Teacher, Inc./Bridgeport, CT

> DEDICATED...
>   ...to Joshua, Emily, Jeremy, Erin, and John...my own family!
>   ...to Dad, Bonnie, and Jana...my "back home" family!
>   ...to Gena, Rachael, and Kristin...my adopted family!
>   ...to Barbara, Cynthia, and Kathy...my family of friends!
>   ...to the First Church of Christ congregation...my church family!
>   ...to "Playgroup-On-The-Green"...my school family!
>   ...to all the great people at First Teacher...my work family!
> and...in memory of Eunice Ruth Russell Burrell, my mom!
>   Sherry Burrell

Copyright © 1991, Sherry Burrell

All rights reserved; except for the inclusion of brief quotations in a review or for classroom use, no part of this book may be reproduced in any form without written permission from the publisher.

The reader is expressly warned to consider and adopt all safety precautions that might be indicated by the activities described herein and to avoid all potential hazards. By following the instructions contained herein, the reader willingly assumes all risks in connection with such instructions.

ISBN 1-878727-05-2

Cover and Page Design: Gene Krackehl
Cover photo: Andrew Brilliant and Carol Palmer (taken at Care-A-Lot Childcare Center, Lexington, MA)
Cover Color: Lisa Schustak

Edited by Helen Strahinich
Editorial Assistant: Jessica Rubenstein
Art Editor: Debby Dixler
Typesetting and Layout: Anita Golton, Beth Ann Bogert

Special thanks from the publisher to Beth Gordon, Thomas Jenen, and Alyssa Levy.

Published by First Teacher Press, First Teacher, Inc.
P.O. Box 29, 60 Main Street, Bridgeport, CT 06602

TABLE OF CONTENTS

Introduction to Families	Teaching Children About Families	4
	Checklist of Concepts	5
The Family-Centered Classroom	The Classroom Family	6
	Discussion Picture	8
	Class Meetings	10
	Rules for our Family at School	12
	Class Job Charts	13
	"Yes, I Can"	14
	Cooperative Games	15
	The Giving Center	16
	Hug Coupons	18
	Class Family Tree	20
My Own Family	Family Portraits	22
	"Meet my Family" Puppets	24
Growth & Change	People Change	26
	Infants for a Day!	27
	The Wise Ones	28
	Life Cycles	29
Families in Nature	Families in Nature	30
	Animal, Vegetable, and Mineral Families	31
	Protecting Our Natural Home	32
	A Family of Ants	33
All Kinds of Families	Family Picture File	34
	Create a Family	35
	Stories with Activities	38
	Family Representations in Books	39
Families Around the World	Families of Many Cultures	41
	Family Culture Days	42
Family/School Interaction	Volunteers in the Classroom	43
	Family Visitors in Class	44
	Family Open House	46
	Tender Loving Care Day	47
	"Celebrate the Family" Picnic	48

TEACHING CHILDREN ABOUT FAMILIES

Every child needs a family—as a source of love, nurturing, and acceptance. All children require positive family experiences to grow and develop into productive, well adjusted adults. They need to understand that any nurturing, loving, supportive group can become a family for them. There are many different kinds of families: blended families, single parent families, traditional nuclear families, and families in which children are cared for by step-parents, surrogate parents, or foster parents. The ideas and activities in this book celebrate many different kinds of families. Learning about the nature of families—what they are and how they function—can increase a child's self-confidence and sense of self-worth.

Find Out What Children Already Know about Families

Before you start a unit on families, it is important to know what children already know about the topic. During circletime, encourage children to talk about families. Use the sample questions that follow as a springboard. Tape record children's discussion. Later, when you listen to the tape, try to evaluate children's understanding of how families work as well as their concerns and misconceptions about families. Try to avoid making judgments about children's comments. Remember that children get ideas about families not only from personal experience but also from books, movies, and TV.

To introduce the family theme, ask children, "What is a family?" Be accepting of children's responses. During this session you want to encourage children to share whatever they think or feel on the subject of families. Follow up with questions, such as:

- "What makes a group of people a family?"
- "Who are the people in a family?"
- "How might a family start?"
- "What things does a family do together?"
- "How do family members help each other?"
- "What happens when family members get angry with each other?"
- "Is it okay for family members to sometimes feel (happy, sad, silly, alone, hurt, etc.)?"
- "Where are some places that families live?"
- "How long do families last?"
- "How do children help in a family?"
- "Can you belong to more than one family?"

How To Use This Book

Adapt the units from this book to meet your specific classroom needs and purposes. Short, independent activities—as well as complete units—can be used in any order or combination throughout the year. Use your discretion and what you know about your children and their families to decide which sensitive topics are appropriate to explore with your group. This is a unique opportunity to create a "classroom family" tailored to your children's needs.

Introduction to Families

CHECKLIST OF CONCEPTS

Before you start a unit on families, review the following checklist. Use it to help you select meaningful issues for your class and to set learning goals. During the course of a unit on families, use the checklist to evaluate children's comprehension of family concepts and to re-assess your goals.

- ❐ The class is a family to which each child makes a contribution.
- ❐ Families work, play, and learn together.
- ❐ Family members help each other and do things together.
- ❐ In a family, all ideas and feelings should have a place to be expressed and heard.
- ❐ Everyone needs and deserves love, acceptance, recognition, nurturing, privacy, and respect from a family.
- ❐ Each family member is unique.
- ❐ Family members care about and appreciate each other.
- ❐ The classroom family and each child's family constitute an extended family.
- ❐ Each family has special qualities to share with the school.
- ❐ People willing to love and support one another make a family.
- ❐ Each family member learns and grows.
- ❐ Families change over time; birth and death are part of the process of change.
- ❐ Exploring families in nature helps us understand our own families.
- ❐ Everyone is a part of the family of nature and of humanity.
- ❐ There are many kinds of families and each one is special.
- ❐ Reaching out to the community enlarges the classroom family.
- ❐ Exploring families of different cultures helps us to understand ourselves.
- ❐ Open communication between home and school builds family feeling.

Making Connections:

Adapt the items from the checklist to use as titles—or themes—for your bulletin board. Or print them on "banners" and place the banners around the room. Read the signs to children. Have children decorate their own "affirmation banners" and march with them in a classroom-family parade.

Introduction to Families   5

THE CLASSROOM FAMILY

Your Class as a Family

Children need to feel safe, secure, and supported in the classroom AT ALL TIMES. This is especially important when they are exploring a subject as sensitive as families. We want our children to feel that they have a caring support group right in the classroom, no matter what the situation at home. By introducing the concept of the classroom family before discussing the child's own family, we offer a way to support and enrich the children's feelings of security.

As teachers, we always want to promote children's self-confidence, their enthusiasm for school, their ability to get along with classmates, and their willingness to express feelings. The challenge for us is to build an environment that promotes these critical goals—a family-style classroom.

First, we need to see **ourselves** as members of the classroom family; we need to work, play, and learn together wth the children as a family; and we need to think of the school as our classroom-family "home." As each "family member" experiences unconditional acceptance, recognition, appreciation, and respect—the total classroom atmosphere benefits. We stop trying to control individuals and start working to create a spirit of family togetherness.

Creating a Family-style Classroom

In a "family-style classroom" all aspects of the environment—room arrangement, physical atmosphere, curriculum planning, and adult roles—are designed to promote children's sense of belonging, independence, confidence, and security. The result is a classroom in which children can relax, explore, and express themselves in productive ways.

To begin to integrate the family theme into your classroom, ask yourself the following questions:

1. Is the child's right to privacy respected?
   - Is there a comfortable place where the child can be alone, if he chooses?
   - Is there a space for each child's possessions and materials?

2. Do lesson plans promote cooperation, togetherness, and group spirit?

The Family-Centered Classroom

THE CLASSROOM FAMILY

3. Does overall planning encourage children to explore feelings? (Or is this limited to one unit on feelings?)
4. Are children responsible for helping to plan, prepare, and clean up on most projects?
   - Are materials and supplies stored within children's reach? 
5. Are activities and the curriculum child-centered?
   - Are activities process-oriented and hands-on?
   - Do activities include sensory stimulation and creativity? 
6. Do adults working in the classroom facilitate, guide, help, ask open-ended questions, stimulate creative problem-solving, and offer support and encouragement? 
7. Is there a center for communication between the "school family" and the child's "home family"?

The Family-Centered Classroom

DISCUSSION PICTURE

CONCEPTS:
- The class is a family to which each child makes a contribution.
- Families work, play, and learn together.
- Family members help each other and do things together.

What You'll Need:
Copies of page 9 • crayons or markers • chart paper pad or chalk board.

Introduction:
Explain that members of a classroom family should help and care for each other. Use the discussion picture on page 9 to introduce and explore with children the idea that they are members of a classroom family.

What to Do:
1. Provide each child with a copy of page 9. You may wish to enlarge the picture with a photo copier for bulletin board use.
2. Encourage children to discuss the picture. Ask: "*How are the people in this picture like a family? How is our class like a family? How can our class be more like a family?*"
3. Have each child choose one person in the picture and color that person.
4. Ask each child to tell a story about that person's best (worst, scariest, funniest) day at school.

Challenge:
- As children tell their stories, write them down. Display their pictures and stories.

Making Connections:
- WE WORK TOGETHER: Decorate a "job box" with children. On index cards, write simple jobs that two children can do together, such as washing the chalkboard or reorganizing the book shelf. The jobs should not be previously assigned on the class job chart. Whenever children volunteer to do a job, send them in pairs to the job box.
- WE PLAY TOGETHER: Cut a two foot square piece out of an old tablecloth or sheet or use a large piece of oaktag. Write the words WE PLAY TOGETHER on it. Give the mat to two or more children and challenge them to cooperatively create something on it. Let them use blocks, puzzles, clay, math manipulatives, or whatever they come up with.
- WE LEARN TOGETHER: This activity helps children focus on what they are learning and on how they are helping others learn. Once a week, ask children to tell you about how they are improving, what they are learning, and how they have helped others to learn. Help children notice their progress. Point out, for example, that they are doing their class jobs without prompting. Sharing your observations will show children that you value their efforts and improvements. Use a chart paper pad or chalkboard to record their responses. Give children paper and markers if they wish to draw their responses.

Read Aloud Books:
- *Will I Have A Friend?* by Miriam Cohen (Macmillan) A new boy at school wonders if he'll ever find a friend.
- *Timothy Goes To School* by Rosemary Wells (Dial) For Timothy, nothing is going well at school, until he discovers Violet.

The Family-Centered Classroom 9

CLASS MEETINGS

Class Meeting Minutes
Date: _____
Today, we discussed
We decided
Next time we will talk about

CONCEPTS:
- The class is a family to which each child makes a contribution.
- In a family, all ideas and feelings should have a place to be expressed and heard.

What You'll Need:
Copies of page 11 • timer • notebook • tape recorder and blank tape • regularly scheduled time once each week.

Introduction:
Class meetings are like "family meetings." The goal of a class meeting might be to generate ideas, to plan projects or field trips, to express positive feelings toward class members, to distribute class jobs, to agree on class rules, or to settle conflicts affecting the group. Explain to children that "class meetings" can make your class more of a family. These few rules may encourage the spirit of democracy:
- Let everyone's viewpoint be heard (one at a time).
- Respect one another's feelings (be polite).
- Accept all ideas without judgment (be encouraging).

What to Do:
1. Call the meeting to order in a formal manner: *"Our classroom meeting is now in session. Let's begin."* A plastic toy hammer makes a great gavel. Set a timer to an agreed upon length of time.
2. Have someone report on the previous meeting using the agenda sheet on page 11. (An adult should have filled it out during that meeting and read it to the reporter.)
3. Encourage children to choose one issue (problem or goal) for discussion. *"Today we've decided to discuss our class rules."*
4. Encourage children to brainstorm suggestions and solutions for each issue, problem, or goal. Accept and write down all ideas.
5. Encourage children to evaluate each suggestion or solution: *"What would we need to carry out this idea? What would happen if we followed this suggestion?"*
6. Work with children to arrive at a consensus. Avoid formal voting that creates a competitive atmosphere.
7. Summarize what has been decided, and get a commitment from children to support that decision: *"Let's try it."*
8. Note new agenda topics, and put them on the schedule for the next meeting.
9. Tell children what a great job they did, and remind them of the next meeting.

Challenge:
- With the help of an adult, let children take turns tape recording the meeting, listening to the recording, and then giving a simple report. (*"We talked about snack. We decided to have a different person put out the napkins each day."*)

Making Connections:
- Videotape a class meeting. Arrange for parents to view the process at a parent-teacher meeting.

Resources for Adults:
- *Discipline Without Tears* by Rudolf Dreikurs and Pearl Cassel (Hawthorne)
- *Maintaining Sanity in the Classroom* by Rudolf Dreikurs et al. (Harper & Row)
- *Teacher Effectiveness Training* by Dr. Thomas Gordon (Wyden)

Class Meeting Minutes

Date: _____

Today, we discussed

We decided

Next time we will talk about

The Family-Centered Classroom

RULES FOR OUR FAMILY AT SCHOOL

CONCEPTS:
- The class is a family to which each child makes a contribution.
- In a family, all ideas and feelings should have a place to be expressed and heard.

What You'll Need:
Large piece of heavy stock paper • cardboard frame (to fit the large piece of paper) • paint, crayons, or markers.

Introduction:
Let children help you create your class rules. When children participate in creating class rules, they are more likely to follow them. Over time, point out positive and negative results of their rules, and encourage children to be flexible with one another. With very young children, simply state a few necessary rules for your classroom. Help them think about why these rules are needed, and what might happen if there weren't any rules.

What to Do:
1. During a class meeting, ask: "*What rules does our classroom family need?*" Have a brainstorming session and accept children's suggestions for class rules. Be flexible, but encourage children to evaluate the consequences of each idea.
2. After children agree on some rules, write them down on the large piece of paper, and follow them for a day (or a week). Later, meet to discuss how the rules are working.
3. Invite children to decorate a cardboard frame for the rules. Post them in a prominent place.

Challenge:
- Provide each child with a photocopy of the rules; let children decorate the paper and take it home to show their parents.

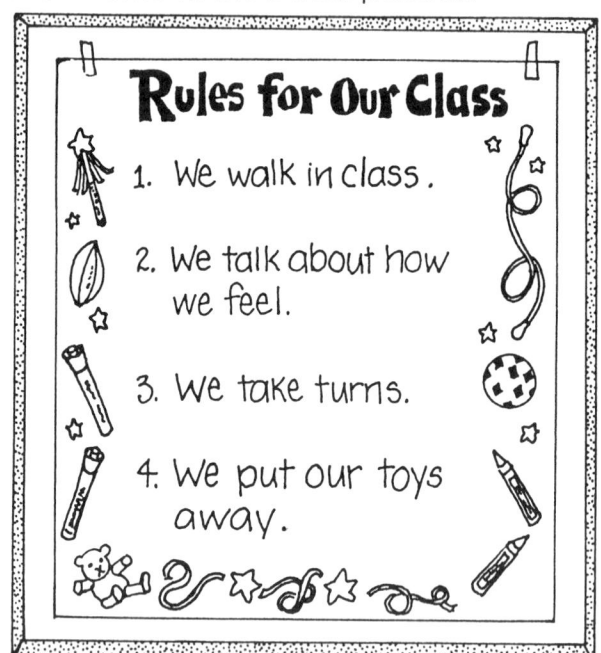

Rules for Our Class
1. We walk in class.
2. We talk about how we feel.
3. We take turns.
4. We put our toys away.

Making Connections:
- With older groups, encourage children to role-play situations to which their rules might apply. Let them discover the consequences.

Read Aloud Books:
- *Herbie's Troubles* by Carol Chapman (E.P. Dutton) If you have bullies at school, here are some ideas to think about.

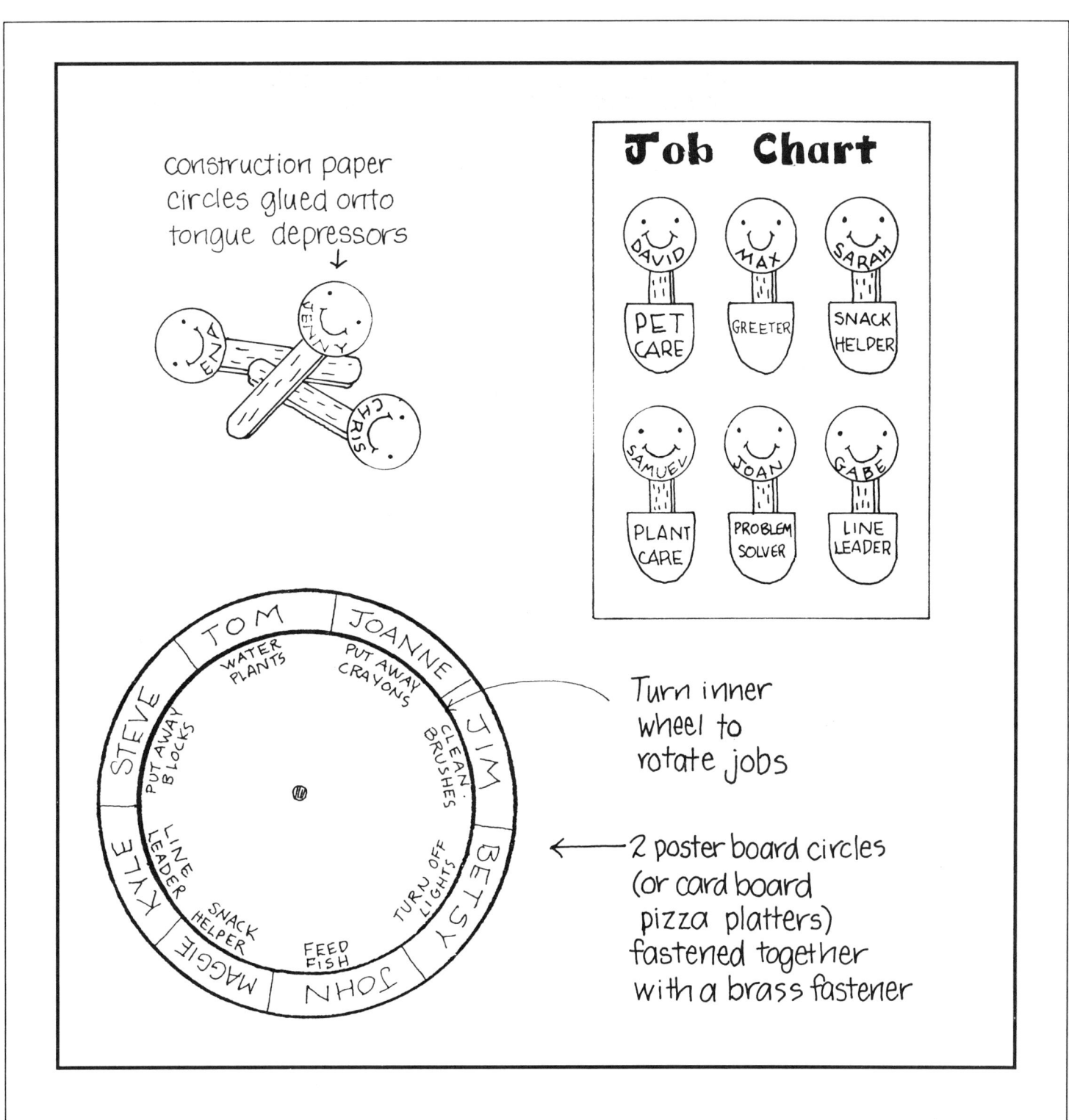

construction paper circles glued onto tongue depressors

Job Chart

DAVID – PET CARE	MAX – GREETER	SARAH – SNACK HELPER
SAMUEL – PLANT CARE	JOAN – PROBLEM SOLVER	GABE – LINE LEADER

Turn inner wheel to rotate jobs

← 2 poster board circles (or card board pizza platters) fastened together with a brass fastener

Class Job Charts:
   Use this page to help you design your own class job chart. You may also want to make "job badges" for each classroom job. Some teachers find that children feel important wearing badges that symbolize their contribution. Assign some creative jobs, such as class greeter, class leader, class time keeper, etc. During a class meeting, discuss ways to rotate chores. Use the chart all year.

The Family-Centered Classroom

"YES, I CAN"

CONCEPTS:
- Everyone needs and deserves love, acceptance, recognition, nurturing, privacy, and respect from a family.
- Each family member is unique.

What You'll Need:
Paper badges • crayons or markers • masking tape • hole puncher • yarn.

Introduction:
Children should recognize and appreciate their talents, strengths, skills, and accomplishments. Celebrate each child's effort, work, and progress.

What to Do:
1. Arrange to talk privately with each child about her positive attributes. Ask questions such as: "*What do you like to do best? What makes you feel proud? What are you good at? What do you work hard at? Think of something that you can do on your own that you used to need help with.*" Write down her answers on a paper badge. Your input will help the child focus on the small accomplishments: buttoning her sweater; pouring her own juice; catching a ball; or putting on her own shoes. Be sure that each child discovers at least three positive things about herself.
2. Give each child her badge. Have the child glue a photo or draw a picture of herself on the badge.
3. Attach the badges to children's clothing or knapsacks with masking tape. Or punch holes, add yarn, and use as necklaces.

write child's name & accomplishment on paper ribbon

Challenge:
- Have children create badges for members of their family or for their friends.

Making Connections:
- TROPHIES:
1. Provide children with a modeling compound that will harden when it dries. Have them form the compound into any trophy shape they choose. When dry, the awards may be painted. Explain to children that you will save the trophies and return them later at a "Court of Awards" ceremony. Present the trophies on a day when children seem to need a confidence boost.
2. Make a sign that states why each child is receiving her award: "*for being here every day this week; for helping a crying friend; for making us smile; etc.*" Attach a sign to each award.
3. When it is time to make the presentation, have the "class leader" of the week (a job on your job chart) present the trophy to each recipient, shake her hand, and say "*Congratulations!*" Take a photo of each recipient with her trophy and her sign, accepting congratulations from the "class leader." Invite parents to attend.

Read Aloud Books:
- *My Hands Can* and *My Feet Can* by Jean Holzenthaler (Dutton) These two photo-packed books celebrate what hands and feet can do.
- *What's Good For a Five-Year Old?* by William Cole (Holt, Rinehart & Winston) Miss Revere prompts children to tell about their interests.

COOPERATIVE GAMES

CONCEPTS:
- The class is a family to which each child makes a contribution.
- Family members help each other and do things together.
- Families work, play, and learn together.

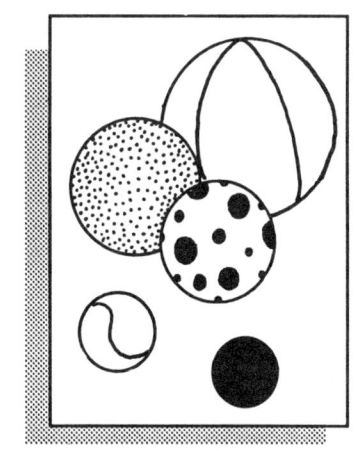

What You'll Need:
Beach balls or other lightweight balls • floor mats or blankets • large paper hearts • other gym equipment.

Introduction:
The themes of interdependence, cooperation, acceptance, sharing, and belonging are all basic to the concept of the family unit. Replacing traditional competitive games (in which children are left out or rejected) with more cooperative games enables children to experience the "family concept."

Games:
- **OVER THE MOUNTAIN:** While singing "The Bear Went Over The Mountain," have children get on their hands and knees and form a chain. They can either link arms with the person next to them or hold onto the ankles of the person in front of them. When all children are connected, they should pretend to be one big bear. Make a "mountain" from a pile of blankets or mats, and have the "group bear" try to get over the "mountain" without children letting go of each other.
- **BLANKETBALL:** Divide children into groups of four or five and provide each group with a blanket. Have each group hold up its blanket so that it can support a beach ball on top. Provide one ball for every two groups. The object is to use the blanket to toss the ball to the other group. That group should then try to catch the ball on top of its blanket. Each group must work together in order to catch the ball and then toss it back to the other group. This game can also be played outside with water balloons.
- **MUSICAL HEARTS:** Instead of chairs, use large paper hearts placed on the floor, one for each child. Have children remove their shoes and march around the hearts to music. When the music stops, everyone must sit or stand on a heart. Before you begin the music again, remove one heart. As you take more and more hearts away, children must fit together on the hearts that are left. That last heart should be the largest, so that children can all fit on it together in one big hug.

Challenge:
- **ARM IN ARM:** Whenever children leave the classroom together—to go to music class, gym, or the auditorium—have them link arms to create cooperative snakes, caterpillars, human ropes, or other animals and objects that allow children to move cooperatively while staying together.

Making Connections:
- **THE STREAMER DANCE:** Give each child a brightly colored scarf or strip of crepe paper. Have children stand in a circle and take the ends of each other's streamers. Play music, and invite children to dance together cooperatively. Have them form a long line and dance around the room, still connected by the streamers. Invite children to tape their scarves or crepe paper strips to a large wall area in any design they choose.

Resources for Teachers:
- *The Cooperative Sports and Games Book* by Terry Orlick (Pantheon) This book is full of great cooperative games for children of all ages.

Introduction:

Children are naturally generous. They will love making cards and wrapping handmade gifts for others (especially for family members or sick friends). They will enjoy thinking of small ways to make others feel special. Likewise, they will benefit from the appreciation they receive for their thoughtfulness. Your class can create a giving center during a holiday season, or anytime. Begin by asking children questions that challenge them to think about the words "give" and "thank." For example: *"What does it mean to give something? What are some of the things you can give? What people do you like to give to? What are some ways you can thank others?"* Accept all ideas. The purpose is to encourage children to share, and to inspire them to make gifts for people they care about.

What You'll Need:

Crayons, colored pencils, or markers • construction paper • shoe boxes or candy boxes • contact paper • gold and silver stickers or glitter • ribbons and bows • sample greeting card signs • collage materials • wrapping paper (sponge-printed newsprint).

THE GIVING CENTER

CONCEPTS:
- Family members care about and appreciate each other.
- The classroom family and each child's family constitute an extended family.

Gifts to Make:
- WRAP IT UP! Any project a child feels good about can become a gift. Have the child wrap it up and add a handmade greeting card.
- GOOD DEED CONTRACTS: During individual conferences, make contracts with children to do a good deed that week. Have each child "sign" his contract. Some good deeds may require practice; for example, learning to set the table.

A "Mission Accomplished" or "Good Deeds" chart or book heightens the fun. Have children report on completed contracts or good deeds done. Write down their good deeds during a special ceremony or give stars, stickers, handshakes, or pats on the back.
- HANDMADE BOOKS AS GIFTS: Make house-shaped pages for "family books," or let each child choose a shape for his book. Help each child to write family facts (names, ages, relationships) on the first page of his book. Give children crayons, colored pencils, or markers to illustrate their books. Have them choose one of the following incomplete sentences for each page, complete each sentence, and add illustrations:

   "The thing I love most about you is...."
   "I loved the time we...."
   "The best part of each day in my family is..."
   "I love my family most when we..."
   "I wish my family would..."

Encourage children to take their books home and share them with their families.

- TREASURE BOX: Ask parents to help you collect shoe or candy boxes. Help each child cover a box with scraps of colorful adhesive-backed contact paper. Give children gold and silver stickers or glitter for their "Treasure Boxes." Help children think of special family-related objects to put inside their boxes.

Read Aloud Books:
- *Hidden Treasure* by Pamela Allen (G.P. Putnam) Two brothers find a treasure. One spends his life hoarding it, while the other discovers a more valuable treasure— love and family.
- *Janet's Thingamajigs* by Beverly Cleary (Morrow) Four-year-old twins fight over Janet's treasures until they grow up.
- *Ask Mr. Bear* by Marjorie Flack (Macmillan) A child who wants to give her mother a birthday present asks the farmyard animals for their ideas.

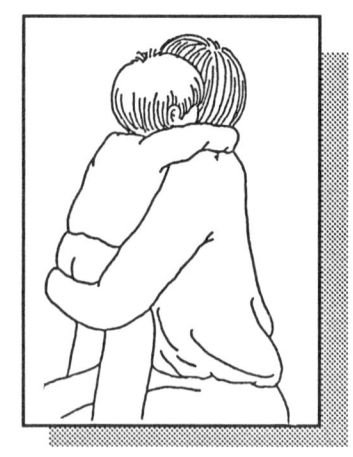

HUG COUPONS

CONCEPTS:
- In a family, all ideas and feelings should have a place to be expressed and accepted.
- Everyone needs and deserves love, acceptance, recognition, nurturing, privacy, and respect from a family.

What You'll Need:
Copies of page 19 • crayons or markers • scissors • ribbon • stickers.

Introduction:
Young children need to be able to express their feelings and have others accept them. In this way, feelings are not regarded as good or bad, or as right or wrong.

Introduce the Hug Coupons to children. Ask children how they might feel about giving a Hug Coupon and how they might feel about receiving one.

What to Do:
1. Provide each child with scissors, crayons, markers, and a copy of page 19.
2. During a class meeting, decide how to distribute coupons to others (give them directly; put them in a "mailbox"; put them on a family member's dinner napkin, etc.).
3. Have children cut the coupons along the heavy lines.
4. Help children read the coupons and discuss how to fill in the blanks with expressions of feelings or "good deeds." (Good for...."one hug"; "some help with folding clothes"; "a back rub"; "ten minutes of quiet time"; etc.)
5. Help children fill in the blanks and draw a picture of the good deed in the box.
6. Help children to roll up each coupon like a scroll and tie it with a ribbon, or to fold each coupon and place in an envelope.

Challenge:
- Place additional copies of the coupons in the Giving Center for children to fill in and use as gifts.

Making Connections:
- FEELINGS CLOCK: Draw a clock on a large piece of oaktag. During a brainstorming session, designate each number on the clock as a different feeling (happiness, sadness, anger, fear, confusion, boredom, peacefulness, amusement, etc.). Indicate each feeling with a simple drawing. Create the pointer for your clock with a brass fastener and an arrow made of oaktag. Encourage children to use the clock to show you their feelings.

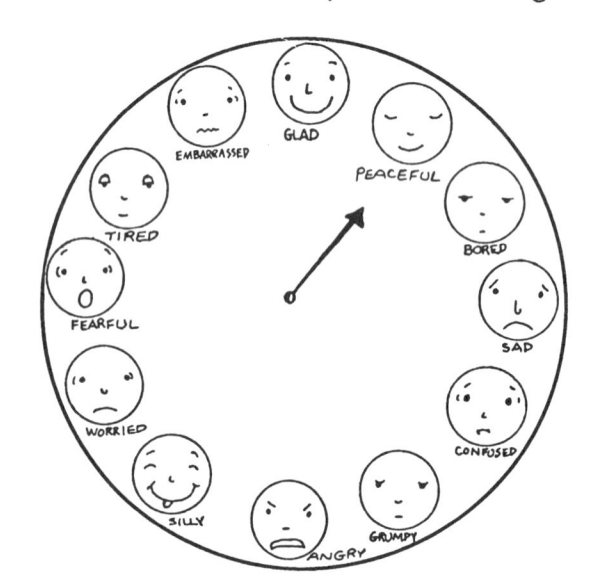

Read Aloud Book:
- *Are You Sad, Mama?* by Elizabeth Winthrop (Harper & Row) What cheers up a little girl's mother quicker than a hug?

18 The Family-Centered Classroom

COUPON

To: _____
From: _____
Good For: _One Hug_ ♡

COUPON

To: _____
From: _____
Good For: _____

COUPON

To: _____
From: _____
Good For: _____

The Family-Centered Classroom

CLASS FAMILY TREE

CONCEPTS:
- The class is a family to which each child makes a contribution.
- The classroom family and each child's family constitute an extended family.

What You'll Need:
A copy of page 21 (enlarged on an overhead projector) • photos or mementos from each child • collage materials for leaves, bark, fruit, etc.

Introduction:
A tree with its roots, a trunk, branches, and leaves is a living, growing, changing system. The classroom family is also a living system—a giant "family tree"—with children, teachers, and children's own families.

What to Do:
1. Using an overhead projector, draw a freehand enlargement of page 21 onto mural paper, and tape it onto a bulletin board or wall.
2. Explain that you are going to make a "class family tree." Tell children that a tree trunk and its roots support and nourish a living tree. Begin with the roots, and tell children that the people who help support the classroom belong there. Fill the roots with photos or mementos (handprints, names, thumbprints, photos, or trinkets) from people such as the director of the center, the secretary, the janitor, the cook, the crossing guard, volunteers, and anyone else who is special to your program.
3. Explain that teachers belong in the trunk of the tree, since they are the leaders who make the "class family tree" grow and flourish. Place photos or other mementos of children's teachers on the trunk itself.
4. Then explain that each child represents a branch on the "class family tree." Draw a branch for each child in the class. Collect photos of each child, and mount them on a backing shaped like a leaf or fruit. Tape each mounted photo onto a different tree branch.
5. Have children glue real tree bark or pretend bark, made from crumpled-up brown tissue paper or scraps of torn construction paper, onto the extra trunk space.

Challenge:
- TAKE-HOME FAMILY TREE: Provide each child with a copy of page 21. Encourage parents to work with children to fill in the names of immediate and extended family members. Send a short note to parents explaining how to use each area of the tree. The roots area should be designated for older friends or relatives who act as a support for the family (grandparents, aunts, uncles, etc.). The trunk area is for the child's role models or immediate guardians (parents, adult friends). The branches should contain the child's name and names of siblings or friends. Suggest that children draw a picture or decorate the area next to each name.

Read Aloud Books:
- *The Giving Tree* by Shel Silverstein (Harper & Row) In this tender parable, a special tree gives a boy many gifts over the years.

The Family-Centered Classroom 21

FAMILY PORTRAITS

CONCEPTS:
- Each family has special qualities to share with the school.
- People willing to love and support one another make a family.

What You'll Need:
A collection of pictures or photos of families • mirror • copies of page 23 • markers or crayons.

Introduction:
When a child creates a visual representation of her family, her pride grows. She understands how special her family is. Show children family portraits by artists (use prints from the library or pictures in books and magazines).

What to Do:
1. Provide each child with a copy of page 23 and markers or crayons. Explain to children that the sheet shows the frame for a family portrait.
2. Have children draw pictures of family members in the frame. Encourage them to include anyone they wish (including pets, caregivers, extended family members).

Challenge:
- A LIVING FRAME: Using a large cardboard box, cut out a six inch frame three feet by two feet. Have children create "living" portraits of themselves by gathering behind the frame, holding the frame up in front of them, and posing. Have a camera handy in order to save the special portraits.

Making Connections:
- FAMILY OF THE WEEK: Assign every child a week. Create a "Family of the Week" bulletin board to be filled by each child during her week. Ask the child to tell about herself and her family. Include her favorite food, favorite trip, favorite game, etc. Accept the child's answers, and display them on the bulletin board. Invite the child to include her family portrait in the display.

☆ **Family of the Week**
Pablo's Family
favorite food: pizza
favorite game: soccer
favorite trip: skiing
favorite season: summer

Notify parents of the date when their family is the "Family of the Week." Invite them to participate in whatever way feels comfortable (sending in a favorite snack; bringing in a family photo album; or visiting the class to help out). Depending on your class, you may want to send home a specific list of ideas so children have comparable displays.

Read Aloud Books:
- *I Go with My Family to Grandma's* by Riki Levinson (Dutton) Five families from different sections of the city travel to visit Grandma. A "Family Portrait" concludes the book.
- *The Berenstain Bears' Not-So-Buried Treasure* by Stan and Jan Berenstain (Random) This story introduces the idea that photographs are valuable mementos of home and family.

My Own Family

My Own Family

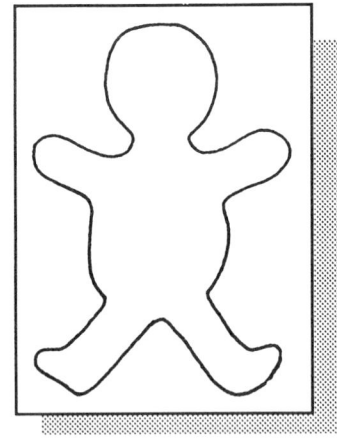

"MEET MY FAMILY" PUPPETS

CONCEPTS:
- Each family has special qualities to share with the school.
- Each family member is unique.

What You'll Need:
Copies of page 25 puppet pattern • paper lunch bags • scissors • yarn, hay, or cotton • 2" photos of family members' faces • glue • crayons or markers • collage materials.

Introduction:
When children understand that their families are special and unique, they carry over their positive feelings into their attitude towards school. They become invaluable classroom family members!

What to Do:
1. Give each child a copy of the puppet pattern on page 25, a paper bag, and scissors. Help children cut out the patterns.
2. Have children glue the patterns to their paper bags.
3. Have children glue a face photo of one of their family members onto the face area of the pattern.
4. Have children add details (yarn, hay, or cotton balls for hair, collage scraps for clothing) to their puppets.
5. Have each child introduce his family member to the class in a simple puppet show. Have children say the puppet's (family member's) name and tell about something he likes to do or say.

Challenge:
- MY FAMILY COLLAGE: Have children draw members of their families on large, heavy paper. Provide magazines, and ask children to cut and paste pictures that remind them of each family member's hobbies, favorite foods, etc.

Making Connections:
- MY FAMILY CALENDAR: Make up a packet of twelve 8 1/2" by 11" calendar pages for each child. Staple the 12 pages (months) together at the top, so each page can be torn off when that month ends. Send the packet home, inviting family members to help their child mark dates that are important to their family. Give each child an 11" by 18" poster board backing. Mount the calendar pages on the bottom half, and add an 8 1/2" by 11" open cardboard frame to the top half. Leave one side of the frame open so children can slide art work in and out. Ask each child to decorate the frame and create a picture to mount into the frame for the first month. Have children make other art works for future months.

Read Aloud Book:
- *My Name Is Emily* by Morse and Emily Hamilton (Greenwillow) This humorous, light-hearted story reminds each child how special she is to her family.

My Own Family

My Own Family   25

PEOPLE CHANGE

CONCEPTS:
- Families change over time; birth and death are part of the process of change.
- Each family member learns and grows.

What You'll Need:
5"x7" oaktag cards or index cards • photos of children (have parents help children find pictures from each year of life) • crayons and markers • string • small hole-puncher • rope • glue.

Introduction:
Individual timelines hung around the room on a rope clothesline will help children see the changes in their own lives and the lives of their classmates from birth to the present.

What to Do:
1. Cut out oaktag cards (5"x7") or use index cards with two holes punched in the top, of each card. Attach cards together with string so they hang horizontally from left to right one after the other.
2. Mark each card Year 1, Year 2, and so on. Have each child bring in pictures from home (one from each year of life) and glue them onto the card or draw pictures depicting themselves in that year of life.
3. Have children dictate a sentence to write on the other side of the card, describing the action or feelings represented in the photo or drawing.
4. Have children share their timelines with the class before hanging them on a rope clothesline across the room. This is a fun, concrete way to experience life changes.

Challenge:
- LIFE-CYCLE COLLAGE: Have children create a long, timeline-like, bulletin board-sized collage from pictures of infants, small children, older children, teens, adults, and the elderly. Let children decide where each picture should be placed along the timeline collage. Make captions describing the pictures.

Making Connections:
- TALKING WITH THE ELDERLY: In a class meeting, have children brainstorm questions they might ask an elderly person: "How was life different when you were my age?" "Tell me about a fun time you had when you were my age." "How have I changed since you've known me?" Have children tell real or made up stories about the elderly people they know.

Read Aloud Books:
- *From Me To You* by Paul Rogers (Orchard) A grandmother tells the story of four generations of family women to her granddaughter.
- *Nonna* by Jennifer Bartoli (Harvey House) This warm-hearted story deals with the sensitive topic of a grandmother's death.

INFANTS FOR A DAY!

CONCEPTS:
- Each family member learns and grows.
- Families change over time; birth and death are part of the process of change.

What You'll Need:
Baby props and baby clothing • a baby photo and a recent photo from every class member (adults and children) • a large bulletin board or wall area • scissors • glue.

Introduction:
Children love to pretend to be babies! Use this interest as a springboard to explore the differences between their behavior today and their behavior as infants. Invite children to talk about what they remember about being babies. Encourage them to share baby pictures, toys, and clothing.

Activities:
- TAKING CARE OF BABY: Set up a "play center" with baby items for dramatic play. Ask parents to help you get old baby clothes, baby blankets, plastic bottles, utensils, toys, stuffed animals, an infant seat, a cradle, an infant swing, a stroller or small carriage, books, small disposable diapers, baby dolls, and rocking chairs. Let children rock baby dolls.
- BABY BATH: Provide children with warm water, small wash cloths, plastic squirt bottles with pretend shampoo (mild dishwashing liquid diluted with water), washable dolls, and towels. Help children learn about hygiene by giving dolls "baby baths."
- BABY VISITORS: If possible, arrange for several real babies to visit the classroom. With children, observe the development of babies at different ages in the areas of eating, movement, language, and playing. Create a book or bulletin board with children's observations.
- WHO'S WHO? Ask parents to send in one baby picture and one recent picture of each child. Mount the baby pictures together in the center of a bulletin board. Include teachers' photos. Put a large border around the baby pictures. Put the recent pictures around the outside of the border, attach a string to each, and challenge children to match them with the baby photos.

Making Connections:
- BABY SHOWER: Have children make pictures, collages, or stories as gifts for a classmate whose family is expecting a baby. Discuss how it would feel to have a new baby in the house. Read books about new siblings. Have children create geometrical designs by pasting black shapes on white paper and vice versa. Help the new big brother or sister attach each design onto a mobile, and let the child bring it home as a gift for the new baby.

Read Aloud Books:
- *Baby Says* by John Steptoe (Lothrop, Lee & Shepard) This touching, realistic story tells about a little boy and how he interacts with his baby brother.
- *Theodore All Grown Up* by Ellen Walsh (Doubleday) Theodore says he's all grown up, so his mom suggests giving away his old toys. (Maybe he's not *all* grown up yet.)

Growth & Change

THE WISE ONES

CONCEPTS:
- Each family member learns and grows.
- Families change over time; birth and death are part of the process of change.

What You'll Need:
Props or clothing of the elderly • crayons or markers • family photos.

Introduction:
Help children become acquainted with senior citizens, and learn to appreciate the elderly. Expose them to elderly visitors and encourage them to collect pictures, stories, and items relating to elderly people in our society.

Activities:
- BE A GRANDPARENT: Encourage families to send in items for the dress-up area that older people might wear (empty eyeglass frames and cases, pocketbooks, fake mustaches and beards, hats, canes, etc.).
- OLDER VISITORS: Invite senior citizens to visit your classroom. Point out to children that "grandparents" come in all ages, shapes, sizes, and colors; and that they have varied interests and backgrounds. Encourage visitors to bring in a personal item to share with children. If possible, arrange for the visitor to do an activity with the class.
- FAMILIES SHARING: Encourage children to find out as much as they can about their grandparents (jobs, homes, hobbies, favorite recipes, traditions). Help children create a bulletin board area for art work, stories, and photos about the senior citizens they know.

Making Connections:
- REACHING IN: Plan a Senior Citizen Appreciation Day with children. Let each child invite one older person—either a grandparent or someone from the community (for resources, contact a nursing home or a local council on aging). Some communities have "foster grandparent" programs, in which the elderly work part time in early childhood classrooms for a small stipend. Ask children to plan a party with the needs of the visitors in mind, and see how thoughtful the youngsters can be!
- REACHING OUT: Visit a nursing home or other program for the elderly. Bring activities (clay, interlocking blocks, crayons, and picture books) that children and the elderly can share together while getting acquainted.

Read Aloud Books:
- *Grandma Gets Grumpy* by Anna Hines (Clarion) When five young cousins sleep over at Grandma's house, they discover that, when pushed far enough, even Grandma gets grumpy!
- *Happy Birthday, Grampie* by Susan Pearson (Dial) Martha's Swedish grandpa, who lives in a nursing home, is blind. For his eighty-ninth birthday, she makes him just the right card.

LIFE CYCLES

CONCEPTS:
- Families change over time; birth and death are a part of the process of change.
- Each family member learns and grows.
- Exploring families in nature helps us understand our own families.

What You'll Need:
Flower seeds or bulbs or grass seed • pots • soil • sponges.

Introduction:
For young children, understanding that their parents and grandparents were once babies may be difficult. However, activities which explore life cycles in the natural world can help them begin to understand this concept.

What to Do:
1. Plant some quick growing flower seeds or bulbs in pots in the classroom, or cut pieces of sponge, dampen, and sprinkle with grass seed.
2. Every few days, have children observe the changes in the plant. Have them draw pictures or help write stories about the daily or weekly changes in the plants.

Challenges:
- CLASS GARDEN: Create a bulletin board garden. Provide magazines and garden catalogs and let each child cut out a picture of a flower, a vegetable, or tree for her space in the garden. Add a baby picture at the roots and a recent photo of the child at the top of her plant. Title the bulletin board OUR CLASS GARDEN.
- HOW MANY? Help children count the number of flowers, trees, and vegetables on the bulletin board. Make a simple bar graph showing how many of each type you have in your "Class Garden."

Making Connections:
- THE CYCLE OF NATURE: Whenever a pet, small animal, or insect enters the classroom, find out as much as you can about the animal's life span, and, if possible, note its age. Have children record with drawings or stories their observations of each animal visitor. Help children learn to respect all living things by returning wild life to its natural habitat as soon as possible.

Read Aloud Books:
- *A Seed Is a Promise* by Claire Merrill (Scholastic). The story illustrates the hopeful idea that in every seed there is a promise "that a new plant will grow."
- *How They Grow*, by Margaret Waring Buck (Abingdon Press) This well-illustrated book follows the stages in the lives of butterflies, toads, turtles, birds, snakes, dragonflies—and more.

Growth & Change

FAMILIES IN NATURE

CONCEPTS:
- Exploring families in nature helps us understand our own families.
- Everyone is a part of the family of nature and of humanity.

What You'll Need:
Nature magazines • scissors • glue • paper • crayons or markers • file folders.

Introduction:
Whatever "family" group you study—animal, vegetable, or mineral—children will soon discover that each individual member is unique. Members of one group may differ in color, behavior, environment, body size, and more. By studying family groups in nature, children will learn about themselves. There are endless variations within each family in nature, including humankind.

What to Do:
1. Provide each child with scissors and a copy of page 31. Have children cut out the pictures along the heavy lines.
2. Talk about the items in each picture and how they are alike. Tell children that the items in the pictures are members of the animal, vegetable, or mineral "families."
3. Let children color the items, paste them on separate pieces of paper, and add new members to each "family," if they wish.
4. Paste one copy of each picture on separate file folders.
5. Give children copies of nature magazines to cut out additional pictures of "family members" and add them to the appropriate folders.

Challenge:
- SORTING CARDS: Select five pictures from each folder and paste them on index cards. Laminate the cards or cover them with clear plastic. Invite children to use the cards to play sorting games.

Making Connections:
- MY OWN TREE: During a nature walk, have each child find a fallen branch (about 12 inches long) for a miniature "tree." On returning to class, have each child put clay in a paper cup, and stand the branch inside. Encourage children to imagine what creatures might live in their "mini-trees," then offer them materials to create houses for those animals. Provide twigs, cotton, yarn, and string for bird nests; black markers to paint on "holes" in the tree for raccoons; or a piece of packing foam for a bee hive. Provide plastic animals or have children create their own from clay or from mounted magazine pictures. Put a sheet of heavy paper under the base of the tree. Have children design this "ground" with rabbit holes, snakes, ants, spiders in grass, or even a small pond for frogs, turtles, and fish.

- THE CLASS TREE: Make a larger (three feet tall) tree for the whole class to decorate. You may wish to turn part of the sandbox area into a "nature community."

Read Aloud Book:
- *The Magic School Bus Inside the Earth* by Joanna Cole (Scholastic). When her students tire of studying animal houses, a teacher announces they will study the earth. The illustrations—of a fantastic field trip collecting rock samples—show how children and teachers work together to learn new things.

Families in Nature   31

PROTECTING OUR NATURAL HOME

CONCEPTS:
- Everyone is a part of the family of nature and of humanity.
- Reaching out to the community enlarges the classroom family.

Introduction:
We belong to the family of nature. Learning about nature should deepen children's appreciation for the natural world. Conclude each nature activity with a discussion about what your class can do to become better "caretakers of the world."

Activities:
- TAKE CARE OF THE EARTH Take children on an "environmental search" around your school. Look for examples of litter and pollution, and decide on class projects to help clean up "your corner of the world." For instance, your class might fill up trash bags with ground litter, make "stop littering" posters, make and distribute lunch-bag-sized litter bags for cars, or write a letter to a local newspaper about air, water, or noise pollution in your area. Teach children about recycling by keeping an empty box in the classroom for used aluminum cans, scrap paper, and cardboard.
- THE WHOLE WORLD IS OURS: Have a sing-along with children. To the tune of "He's got the whole world in his hands," sing "We've got the whole world in our hands," and decide how the class can help keep it clean.

Have children clap the beats or stamp their feet as they learn the words to this poem, "This Is Your World" by Sherry Burrell:

This is your world. It takes care of you.
Your friends are special. You are special to them too.
This is your world. It takes care of you.
Your parents love you. Your teachers care about you too.
This is your world. Keep it clean and safe and strong.
Cause if you don't care, everything will turn out wrong.
The birds will die off. Lakes will dry and disappear.
The trees and flowers will stop growing through the year.
Nature surrounds us. She provides us with our food.
We must respect her, replacing everything we use.
With lots of thinking, we can save the earth.
We'll look to nature, to teach us new ways of re-birth.
This is your world. It takes care of you.
And if we all care, we will take care of it too!
Add: *This is (child's name) world, it takes care of (him/her),too.*
He/she (plants a garden/saves old bottles/picks up litter),
And that's a special thing to do!

Read Aloud Books:
- *Berenstain Bears and the Coughing Catfish* by Stan and Jan Berenstain (Random House). The bears figure out what to do about pollution.
- *Barbapapa's Ark* by Annette Tison and Talus Taylor (Xerox Educ. Publications). With amusing and colorful illustrations, this book shows how human pollution can foul up the world.

A FAMILY OF ANTS

CONCEPTS:
- Exploring families in nature helps us understand our own families.
- Everyone is a part of the family of nature and of humanity.

What You'll Need:
A large, clear unbreakable jar (at least quart-size) • sugar cubes, wheat germ, grass seeds, dead insects, bread crumbs, or chopped meat • a square, 1/2-inch piece of sponge • a piece of screen • a piece of black construction paper • a collection of books on animal and insect families.

Introduction:
By examining the organization of different "families" in nature, children learn to appreciate and respect all kinds of families. Watching ants work together to build their home and transport food underlines the need for cooperation in families.

What to Do:
1. Take children on a nature walk. Locate a large, active ant hill. Avoid dangerous breeds of ants.
2. Dig up as much of the ant hill as possible, and place it into the jar. Leave a small space at the top.
3. Have children gather leaves and grass from an area near the hill. Place their pickings into the top of the jar.
4. Feed ants a sugar cube, or sprinkle wheat germ, grass seed, dead insects, bread crumbs, or chopped meat on the soil.
5. Saturate a 1/2 inch square piece of sponge with water, and place it on top of the soil in the jar. Be sure to keep the sponge moist.
6. Cover the jar with a piece of screen.
7. Tape black construction paper around the jar to create a dark underground environment. Take paper off when children want to view the paths and rooms the ants have built. Remind children that the ant's house will fall in if they shake the jar.

Challenge:
- CLASS PLAY: After children have become familiar with ant families, put on a class play. Help children make ant costumes with paper grocery bags and pipe cleaners and dramatize what they have learned about the roles of ant family members.

Making Connections:
- ANIMALS AND INSECT FAMILIES: Choose an animal or insect—for example, wolf, chimpanzee, beaver, rabbit, lion, fish, bee, or cat—to study in depth. Ask your librarian for well illustrated, non-fiction books that describe the animal's habitat, food sources, care of young, family system, and general lifestyle. During the course of your study, challenge children to find similarities between the animal's family and human families.

Read Aloud Books:
- *Two Bad Ants* by Chris Van Allsburg (Houghton Mifflin). Read children this story of an ant's day in a kitchen.
- *Ant Cities* by Arthur Dorros (Crowell). This terrific story reveals the secrets of an ant's life.
- *Insects That Live In Families* by Dean Morris (Raintree) This "let's read and find out" book is about bees and ants.

FAMILY PICTURE FILE

CONCEPTS:
- Each family member is unique.
- People willing to love and support one another make a family.

What You'll Need:
Magazines • art books • scissors • construction paper • file folders or envelopes.

Introduction:
When children are exposed to different kinds of families, they begin to accept and appreciate differences that exist in the world around them. To the child that means: "*My family is special!*"

What to Do:
1. Collect used magazines from friends, yard sales, and parents. Include magazines which focus on plant and animal families. Find reproductions of famous paintings of families in art books or catalogs and make photo copies. Try to locate pictures that show people of different races, economic classes, and nationalities. Include different kinds of families—single-parent families, dual-parent families, and families without children; as well as families that include grandparents, families in group homes, and families with members with different hairstyles, body types, or physical capabilities.
2. Have children look through magazines and cut out pictures of families. Have them create a "picture file" by mounting each one on a brightly colored piece of construction paper, and dictating a caption for you to write under each picture. Display pictures on a bulletin board. When the bulletin board is taken down, have children sort the pictures into separate envelopes or folders (by whatever divisions you choose) for future use.

Challenge:
- IMAGINARY FAMILIES: On a pleasant day, have children lie on their backs outside and create an imaginary family for themselves in the sky. Ask children to imagine themselves living in a kingdom above the clouds where they are members of a magical family of people, animals, plants, or stars. Have children close their eyes and visualize their magical families. Ask children: "*What does your home look like? Imagine you are having a meal with your new family—who is there? What sounds do you hear? What smells so good? What tastes do you notice?*" Then tell children it's time to say good-bye to their imaginary homes. Have them open their eyes. When you return to the classroom, ask children to draw pictures and/or tell stories about their "imaginary families."

Making Connections:
- FAMILIES IN BOOKS: Whenever children find a story they enjoy, ask about how the families in the book interact, and then re-read it. Help children describe the different kinds of families they encounter.

Read Aloud Books:
- *Families* by Meredith Tax (Little, Brown & Co.) As a general resource, this book helps expand the child's idea of a family.
- *All Kinds of Families* by Norma Simon (Albert Whitman & Co.) This book describes many patterns of family life.

CREATE A FAMILY

CONCEPTS:
- Families work, play, and learn together.
- There are many kinds of families and each one is special.

What You'll Need:
Pipe cleaners • spoons • sequins • feathers.

Introduction:
Tell children, *"The right kind of family is YOUR kind of family."* In a healthy family, people care for and nurture one another. Recognizing this, encourage children to acknowledge and accept families different from their own. Creating "new, original" families based on their fantasies will increase children's understanding and respect for the differences.

What to Do:
1. Offer a range of materials or activities (one at a time) following the suggestions on pages 36 and 37.
2. Have children use the materials to create families never seen before. They may use clay to invent a family of three children with no adults. Or they may create a family with a pipe cleaner "mommy," two spoon "daddies," and a feather-and-sequins "monster" child!
3. Ask children to tell about their fantasy families. "Who are the members? What are their names? How do they spend their days? What kinds of things do they like to do?"

Challenges:
- **FINGERTIP FAMILY:** Provide a light-colored rubber glove for each child. Have the child use a pen to draw a face and body on each finger of the glove. Have children wear the gloves and recite familiar finger plays or make up new ones.
- **MOBILE OF FAVORITES:** Have each child tell about, bring in, or cut out pictures of things that remind him of family favorites (favorite color, toy, book, place, song, sport, etc.). Mount the pictures (written words, trinkets) on heavy stock paper or oaktag, punch a hole in the top, attach string or yarn of different lengths to each piece, and tie each child's favorites onto a separate coat hanger. Tie a clothesline across the room, and hang up all the coat-hanger mobiles. Choose one topic and create a graph of favorites (Our Favorite Foods).

Making Connections:
- **COLOR FAMILIES:** Ask children if they think that colors belong in families. Accept their answers. Give children paint sample strips and have children cut them out into individual colors, sorting and re-sorting them into "color families." Invite children to draw faces on the individual color strips.

Read Aloud Books:
- *Of Colors and Things* by Tana Hoban (Greenwillow) This wordless book full of brilliant-colored photos invites children to see "color families" on each page.
- *Color Zoo* by Lois Ehlert (Lippincott) Ingeniously crafted, this book creates a new animal picture on each page.

All Kinds of Families

Paper Cup People

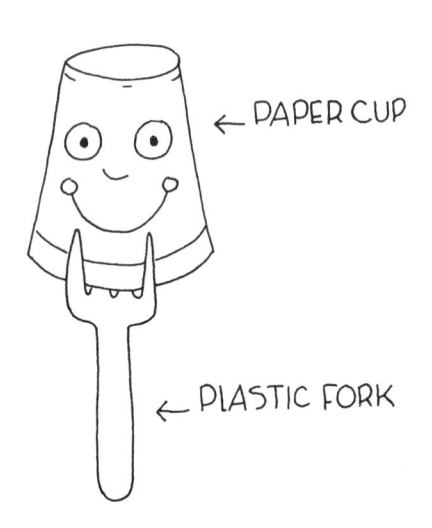

← PAPER CUP

← PLASTIC FORK

Paper Plate People

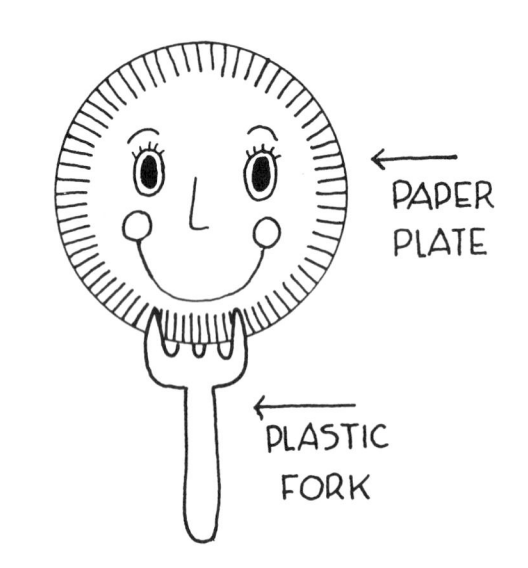

← PAPER PLATE

← PLASTIC FORK

Paper Plate Puppet People

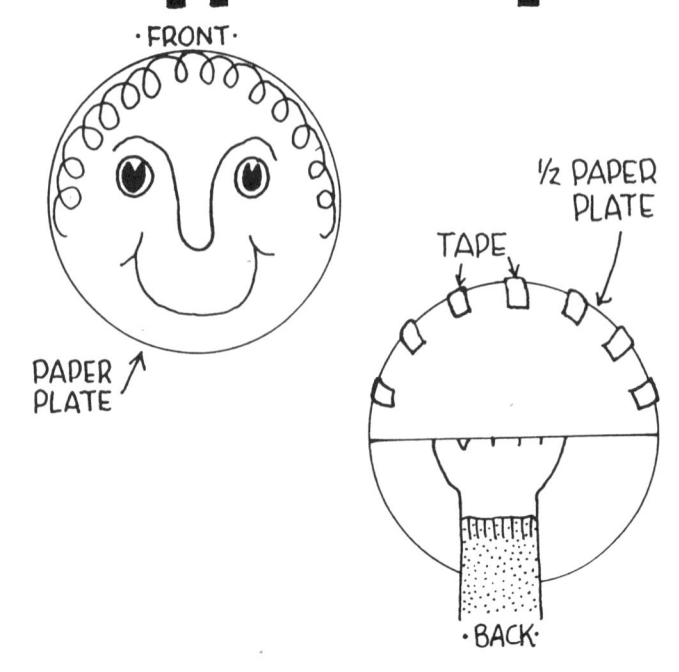

·FRONT·

PAPER PLATE

TAPE

½ PAPER PLATE

·BACK·

Spoon People

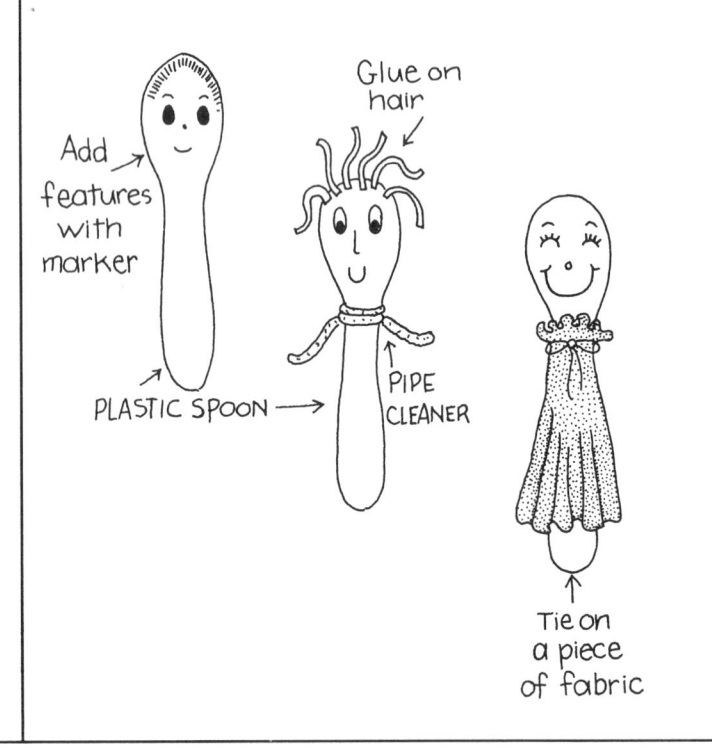

Add features with marker

PLASTIC SPOON →

Glue on hair

PIPE CLEANER

Tie on a piece of fabric

36   All Kinds of Families

Tongue Depressor People

Draw features on tongue depressors

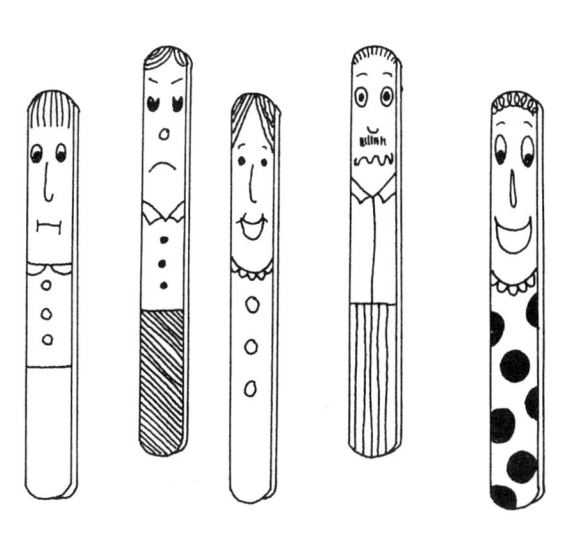

Plastic Egg People

WHAT YOU'LL NEED:
- PLASTIC EGG-SHAPED HOSIERY CONTAINER
- YARN (FOR HAIR)
- PEBBLE OR PIECE OF CLAY
- GLUE
- PERMANENT MARKERS

WHAT TO DO:

1. Open the plastic container and glue pebble to bottom
2. Decorate with markers to make face and body
3. Push it over – and it returns to a stable position

Yarn People

WHAT YOU'LL NEED:
- YARN (DIFFERENT COLORS)
- 6" PIECE OF CARDBOARD
- PIPE CLEANERS
- BITS OF LACE
- PIECE OF AN OLD SCARF
- ARTIFICIAL FLOWERS
- FABRIC SCRAPS

WHAT TO DO:

1. Wrap yarn around and around a 6" piece of cardboard. Tie and knot a piece of yarn around the top of the yarn loops then slip off the cardboard.
2. Tie another piece of yarn far enough down to form a head.
3. Insert arms. Arms maybe smaller yarn loops or pipe cleaners.
4. Then, tightly tie another piece of yarn around the middle for the waist.
5. The remainder can be left as is for a skirt or divided and tied into legs.
6. Fabric skirts, bits of lace, a scarf for the head or small, artificial flowers can be used to give the doll personality.

Glove People

Glue felt, fabric, yarn, feathers onto finger tips of a glove. Use whole glove or cut apart for finger puppets.

All Kinds of Families

STORIES WITH ACTIVITIES

CONCEPTS:
- Each family member is unique.
- People willing to love and support one another make a family.

Introduction:
Books can be springboards to many meaningful, creative experiences. Use the following books and activities to help children explore different kinds of families.

Books and Activities:

Alexander and the Terrible, Horrible, No Good, Very Bad Day by Judith Viorst (Scholastic). Alexander, the youngest of three boys in his family, has had a miserable day.

Have children make their own books by drawing pictures and telling about things that happened to them on a special kind of day. Talk about how they could make someone having a "terrible, horrible day" feel better.

If You Listen by Charlotte Zolotow (Harper). A little girl misses her father, who has been away a long time. Her understanding mother offers her a way to hold him in her heart.

During a quiet time, help children imagine unusual "sounds" they might "listen" to (imagine, for instance, the sound of the sunset, a wildflower, softness, or light).

One More Thing, Dad by Susan Thompson (Albert Whitman). Caleb is getting ready to go out to play. He counts the nine items he plans to take with him, then decides that the tenth item should be his dad.

Challenge children to cut and paste, draw pictures of, or collect (in a box, suitcase, or backpack) nine items they'd like to bring with them to play. Ask what their "tenth item" would be.

A Place For Ben by Jeanne Titherington (Greenwillow). Ben's brother's crib is moved into his room. While creating a space of his own, Ben learns that privacy can be lonely.

Provide sheets, blankets, and boxes, and let children make use of tables, corners, and climbers as well. Encourage them to create private spaces in the classroom, spend quiet (rest) time in their own spaces, then visit each other. Talk about feelings that arise.

Sometimes I Have To by David Ridyard (Gareth Stevens). This book describes some things children are told they should or should not do. Discussion pages are included.

Challenge children to add their own ideas to those in the book. Make a chart or graph of "shoulds" and "shouldn'ts." Add up children's suggestions.

Why Am I Different? by Norma Simon (Albert Whitman). While raising some controversial issues, this wonderful book celebrates the uniqueness of every child and her special family.

Have children create their own "Why I Am Different" book. The pages might include sentence stems for children to finish: *"I feel big when..." "I feel small when..." "I'm good at..." "For my birthday, I wish..." "My family is special because..."* and ending with *"I am different because..." "and that makes me a VERY SPECIAL PERSON!"*

All Kinds of Families

FAMILY REPRESENTATIONS IN BOOKS

CONCEPTS:
- There are many kinds of families and each one is special.
- People willing to love and support one another make a family.

What You'll Need:
Books • a comfortable book area.

Introduction:
Books can help us to find out more about ourselves and our world. There are many books with family themes. Others have family-related themes. Encourage imaginative thinking about each story. As you read, help children to observe family interactions and notice family themes.

Books:
- *Adopted* by Judith Greenberg and Helen Carey (Franklin Watts). This book with great photos teaches that each child is special.
- *Amifika* by Lucille Clifton (Dutton). Amifika's Daddy is coming home from the army. Mama plans to get rid of something in the house to make room. Amifika worries if Mama is going to throw him out.
- *Being Adopted* by Maxine Rosenberg (Lothrop). This photo-filled book follows three families who adopted children with racial and cultural roots different from their own.
- *Black Is Brown Is Tan* by Arnold Adoff (Harper & Row). This poetic story about everyday life portrays a racially mixed family.
- *A Chair for My Mother* by Vera Williams (Greenwillow). After her family's house burns down, a little girl, her mother, and grandmother rebuild their lives.
- *Daddy* by Jeannette Caines (Harper & Row). How does a little girl who visits her Daddy every Saturday fit into his life?
- *Darlene* by Eloise Greenfield (Methuen). The story of Darlene (who uses a wheelchair) shows the frustration of always having to wait.
- *Everett Anderson's 1, 2, 3* by Lucille Clifton (Holt, Rinehart and Winston). Everett likes being alone or with Mommy. He's not sure he wants a new man in the family.
- *Everett Anderson's Nine Month Long* by Lucille Clifton (Holt, Rinehart and Winston). This poetic story tells about an Afro-American family with a little boy, his pregnant mom, and her new husband.
- *Grandmother* by Jeannie Baker (Andre Deutsch). This story describes a child's day with her old grandmother at her old house.
- *Here I Am, an Only Child* by Marlene Fanta Shyer (Charles Scribner). This story shows the advantages and disadvantages of being an only child—with the plusses winning out.
- *I Have a Sister; My Sister Is Deaf* by Jeanne Whitehouse Peterson (Harper & Row). Black and white drawings reinforce an interesting text.
- *It's Mine!* by Alicia Garcia deLynam (Dial). Beautiful water colors illustrate a preschooler's love for and rivalry with his toddler sibling.
- *Lisa and the Grompet* by Patricia Coombs (Lothrop, Lee & Shepard). Lisa is sad and angry because she is constantly told what to do. When she runs off and meets a grompet, she finds out that he is sad and angry because no one tells him what to do!

All Kinds of Families

FAMILY REPRESENTATIONS IN BOOKS

CONCEPTS:
- There are many kinds of families and each one is special.
- People willing to love and support one another make a family.

Books:

- *Matthew and His Dad* by Arlene Alda (Little Simon). Black and white photos show the many sides of a father-son relationship.
- *Monster and the Baby* by Virginia (Albert Whitman). A little monster tries to get baby-sister monster to stop crying.
- *Moon Tiger* by Phyllis Root (Holt). Jessica is angry at her little brother when she dreams of a tiger who offers to eat him up.
- *My Brother Steven Is Retarded* by Harriet Sobel (Macmillan). Eleven-year-old Beth tells about her little brother.
- *My Friend Leslie* by Maxine Rosenberg (Lothrop). This photo book tells the story of a handicapped kindergarten-aged child.
- *My Hands, My World* by Catherine Brighton (Macmillan). Maria, who is blind, uses her ears, her hands, and her nose to see the world.
- *My Little Foster Sister* by Muriel Stanek (Whitman). An "only child" adjusts to having a foster sister, and then has to say good-bye.
- *My Mom Needs Me* by Mildred Walker (Lothrop). When the new baby arrives, a little boy feels he shouldn't go out to play.
- *My Mom Travels a Lot* by Caroline Fellen Bauer (Frederick Warne & Co.). What is it like to have a mother who travels?
- *My Mommy's Special* by Jennifer English (Children's Press). A little girl tells about her mom, who uses a wheelchair to get around.
- *My Sister's Silent World* by Catherine Arthur (Children's Press). This book describes what life is like for a deaf child.
- *One of the Family* by Peggy Archer (Western). When a new baby joins a family of six, she had better like noise.
- *Our Family Vacation* by Denise Burt (Gareth Stevens). Luis and his family take a two-week summer vacation at the beach.
- *Rajesh* by Curt and Gita Kaufman (Macmillan) This moving book tells about a boy missing both legs and one hand.
- *Sara Loves Her Brother* by Ruth Hooker (Albert Whitman). Spend a day with Sara (a preschooler) and find out how much she loves to be with her brother!
- *Someone Special Just Like You* by Tricia Brown (Holt). This book shows handicapped children doing everything children love to do!
- *Something Is Going to Happen* by Charlotte Zolotow (Harper). Watch what happens in the life of one family after a new snowfall.
- *Stevie* by John Steptoe (Harper). Robert is an only child—until his mom starts babysitting for another little boy.
- *The Berenstain Bears* series by Stan and Jan Berenstain (Random House). This series offers a variety of stories about family relationships.
- *The New Baby At Your House* by Joanna Cole (Morrow). This simple book shows how siblings deal with new babies.
- *The Not-So-Wicked Stepmother* by Lizi Boyd (Viking Kestrel). Hessie is about to meet her new stepmother. Are the stories she's heard about stepmothers really true?
- *Tight Times* by Barbara Shook Hazen (Viking). This story tells about a boy who longs for a dog while his family faces "tight times."

All Kinds of Families

FAMILIES OF MANY CULTURES

CONCEPTS:
- Exploring families of different cultures helps us to understand ourselves.

Introduction:
Sharing stories about families from all around the world deepens children's appreciation for the variety of people who are our neighbors.

Books:

- *Brothers: A Hebrew Legend* retold by Florence Freedman (Harper). When a dying father divides his land between his two sons, their efforts remind us how to be fair.
- *A Drop Of Honey* by Djemma Bider (Simon & Schuster). An Armenian tale about a girl whose quarrel with her brothers leads to trouble. The book includes a baklava recipe.
- *In My Mother's House* by Ann Nolan Clark (Viking). A collection of rhythmic stories, this book tells of the Tewa Indian children of Tesuque Pueblo, near Santa Fe, New Mexico.
- *In the Land of Small Dragon* told by Dang Manh Kha to Ann Nolan Clark (Viking) This poetic Vietnamese Cinderella tale is an enchanting read-aloud story for quiet time.
- *Katie Morag and the Two Grandmothers* by Mairi Hedderwick (Little, Brown). Set in Scotland, this story tells of Katie's two grandmothers who don't like each other very much.
- *Madeline* stories by Ludwig Bemelmans (Viking). The adventures of the youngest and naughtiest little girl in a Paris orphanage will delight children.
- *My Grandmother's Cookie Jar* by Montzalee Miller (Price/Stern/Sloan). Every time she offers a cookie, a child's grandmother has a story about their Native American heritage. When Grandma dies, the child realizes that her cookie jar will always be filled with Grandma's love and her Native American spirit.
- *The Weaving of a Dream* retold by Marilee Heyer (Viking Kestrel). This beautifully illustrated Chinese folktale tells the story of an old woman who fears she will die if one of her sons can't retrieve her stolen brocade.
- *Tony's Bread* by Tomie dePaola (G.P. Putnam). Pride, courtship, and cunning lead to the invention of sweet "panettone" bread in this Italian folktale.
- *Where Children Live* by Thomas Allen (Prentice-Hall). Each two-page spread illustrates a different part of the world, and a short description tells where the children live.

Making Connections:
- FAMILIES AROUND THE WORLD: Find a way to start a "picture-pal" exchange with a class from another country. Inquire with international or religious organizations (Association for Childhood Education International, 11141 Georgia Ave., Suite 200, Wheaton, MD 20902). Ask parents if they would like to exchange names with parents from another country—and watch the letters, pictures, and love grow!

FAMILY CULTURE DAYS

CONCEPTS:
- Exploring families of different cultures helps us to understand ourselves.

Introduction:
No matter where a family lives or what its cultural roots may be, it is unique. Celebrate ethnic diversity in your classroom. Celebrate differences!

Plan a day of food, games, songs, props, stories, art activities, and costumes reflecting a specific culture. **Historical Days** (Frontier Day, Early American Settler Day, the First Olympics Day, 1920's Day, or a 1950's Day) or **Ethnic Days** (German Day, Puerto Rican Day, Irish Day, Russian Day, Chinese Day, Native American Day, Italian Day, African Day, etc.) are meaningful when families with common heritages work together to plan the celebration. If a school-wide celebration is feasible, each classroom could present a different "cultural experience"—and children can celebrate by moving from room to room.

What to Do:
1. Decide whether your celebration will occur during school, in the evening, or over a weekend. Send home a note explaining your intention to celebrate the cultural diversity of the children in your class. Include a questionnaire to find out about the origins of each child's family members. Ask for information about ethnic recipes, language, holidays, and customs. Encourage families to bring in heirlooms or objects to show to the class. Also ask about cultural stories, books, games, songs, music, costumes, or dances. Adapt the questionnaire to reflect your community.
2. After enlisting the support of children's families, assign appropriate activities to each family.
3. If your class is culturally homogeneous, turn to the staff or community for cultural diversity (crossing guard, principal, cook, janitor, or local business people).
4. Keep in mind that there is no correct way to proceed with this activity. The only guideline is to stimulate children's interest, acceptance, and respect for all cultures and all people.

Challenge:
- POTLUCK: Invite each family to bring in a potluck dish for a school "family" gathering. Ask for salads, entrees, and desserts. Encourage parents to let children help prepare a dish from their heritage—or one they enjoy.

Making Connections:
- SONG & GAME FEST: Invite each family to share a game or song from their own heritage or from another culture they enjoy.

Read Aloud Book:
- *A Visit with Grandma* by Sharon Hart Addy (Albert Whitman & Co.). This story of a little girl who bakes strawberry kolach with her great-grandma includes a recipe. It will give children the feeling of a visit with an elderly Czechoslovakian woman.

Families Around the World

VOLUNTEERS IN THE CLASSROOM

CONCEPTS:
- The classroom family and each child's family constitute an extended family.
- Open communication between home and school builds the family feeling.

Introduction:
Rewarding experiences occur when the classroom family opens itself to the home family. Parent volunteers may become valuable class-family members. Be sure to carefully screen all people who will be interacting with children.

Types of Parent Volunteers:
Parents may volunteer to help out in the classroom for many different reasons. They come into your classroom with different levels of experience, expertise, and a variety of personal needs. Interview each parent volunteer before assigning him a job. Be sure that volunteers understand your philosophy and needs. Here are some reasons why volunteers may offer their help, and some suggestions for how to respond:

- Some parents volunteer just because they love children. Give these people a limited amount of supervised time working on a prepared activity with a few children (reading stories to children or helping children write stories during "center time").
- Some parents volunteer because they want to feel useful. Have these volunteers help with filing, typing, cooking, preparing craft materials, or working with children—depending on their interests and skills.
- Some parent volunteers want to gain work experience or to find out general career information about childcare. Expose them to different aspects of childcare. Have them come at various times of the day to help out. Be sure to explain the scope of each job. This is also an opportunity to screen future childcare workers.
- Some parents volunteer because they want to see how their children behave in class. Explain that children sometimes behave very differently when their parents are present. Talk with the parent about this before and and after the visit.
- Some parent volunteers have a skill, talent, or background they would like to share. Welcome them! Take some time to help these parents with the "how-tos" of presenting to children.

Making Connections:
- JOB FILE: Create a job file with a file box and index cards. Whenever you find a job that needs to be done, (and you just don't seem able to get to it regularly), add it to the job file. Then, when a parent volunteer shows up, look through the box (or have them look), and choose a job you both agree would meet everyone's needs. Include things that always need re-doing (like cleaning the easel, helping children write stories, etc.).

Reminder:
Be sure to remind children that a volunteer is a visitor in their classroom. Help volunteers to feel welcomed and accepted. Introduce them to the children, have children greet them, encourage children to offer them gifts (from the Giving Center), and teach children to thank volunteers for their services.

Family/School Interaction

FAMILY VISITORS IN CLASS

CONCEPTS:
- Open communication between home and school builds family feeling.

What You'll Need:
Copies of page 45 • crayons or markers.

Introduction:
It's beneficial to both parents and children when family members visit the class. Having visitors gives children a chance to practice greeting them, using good manners, making introductions, and being good hosts.

What to Do:
1. Have a few children make personalized invitations for family members to visit your class. Use a copy of page 45 as a base.
2. Send a personal note to the invited guest explaining the reasons for and expectations of the visit. Children can learn about different careers from adults in the extended "classroom family." Ask guests to bring their "tools of the trade," and to wear a uniform, if appropriate.
3. Contact the person by telephone to arrange a date and time. Mark the classroom calendar with the date of the visit.
4. Enlist the person's help in teaching children how to treat visitors in their classroom. On your class job chart, assign "visitor's day jobs" to children. Here are possibilities:
   - One child could greet the visitor (as a representative of the class) by shaking hands, and saying something like, "Hello, _____, my name is _____, and our class welcomes you!" This child or another might also say, "Good-bye and thank-you for coming!" when it is time for the person to leave.
   - One child might be assigned to take the visitor's coat, hang it up, and retrieve it when the visitor is about to leave.
   - Another child might show the visitor around the room.
   - Someone could get the visitor a chair.
   - Someone might offer the visitor a snack.

Challenge:
- INTERVIEWING: During circletime or a class meeting, generate a list of questions children would like to ask a visitor to your class. Brainstorm a general list of questions for visitors. It's fun to use a big doll as a pretend visitor in order to help children generate ideas. Include specific, "close-ended" questions that can be answered with a single word or piece of information ("*What is your name? What do you do? Where do you live?*" and "open-ended" questions that require a more thoughtful explanation ("*How is your job interesting? Why are you visiting us today?*"). Let children practice interviewing each other and a teacher before interviewing a visitor.

During each visitor interview, have an adult write (on a large chart) what the class learns about the visitor.

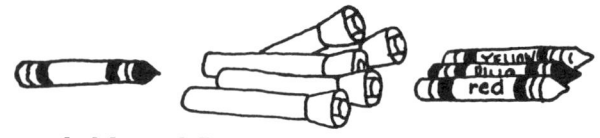

Read Aloud Books:
- "*I Can Be a...*" books (Children's Press) is a series of books that offers a non-sexist approach to careers. Each book begins with a picture dictionary showing materials associated with the job. Ensuing text and photos show men and women in each career.

44 Family/School Interaction

To a: _____
Date: _____
Place: _____

PLEASE COME!

You Are Invited

FAMILY OPEN HOUSE

CONCEPTS:
- Open communication between home and school builds family feeling.

What You'll Need:
Copies of page 45 • crayons, colored pencils, paints, or markers • collage materials • large paper hearts.

Introduction:
When the child's family feels welcomed into the school, everyone benefits from better understanding and improved relationships.

What to Do:
1. Schedule a date and time for a school "open house." Parents could come alone or with children. (Children love to come, but not every school has enough space for everyone.) Children love to plan this event. Ask them to choose their favorite activity for each learning center. Then they can help prepare and set up each area with these activities for their guests. Also, children could prepare a special snack for the guests.
2. Fill in one copy of the invitation on page 45 with the appropriate information (date, time, etc.) and cut along the heavy line. Then make multiple copies.
3. Provide each child with as many copies of page 45 as needed (one per guest) and crayons, markers, and other art media.
4. Have children color and design the invitations to bring home to their families.
5. During the open house, let parents do the activity in each of the prepared centers. Have them follow their child's daily schedule (in shortened form), experiencing circletime, learning centers, snack time, music and movement, etc. Use this opportunity to explain the goals and expectations for each part of the child's day. When the parents get home, they can answer their *child's* question, *"What did you do at school today?"*

Suggested Activities:
- Circletime: Have a class "family" meeting with parents (see pages 10–11).
- Art area: Family puppets (see pages 24–25).
- Science area: Sort animal, vegetable, and mineral cards and/or create lotto games with them (see pages 30–31).
- Music time: Make up movements for "This Is your World," substituting children's names and how they care for the world. (see page 32).
- Snack time: Have a family potluck snack (see page 42), or create a family recipe book by trying to write out family recipes from memory.
- Language: Make "Yes I Can" badges (see page 14).
- Motor Skills: Play Blanketball (see page 15).
- Dramatic Play: Infants for a Day (see page 27).
- Giving Center: Make cards or gifts for a family member, relative, or friend (see pages 16-17).

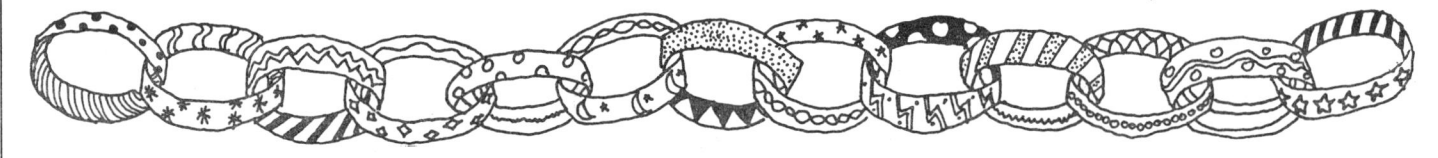

Family/School Interaction

TENDER LOVING CARE DAY

CONCEPTS:
- Each family has special qualities to share with the school.

(Invitation card: To:___ Date:___ Place:___ PLEASE COME!)

What You'll Need:
Copies of page 45 • markers or crayons • tools and equipment • 3" x 5" index cards • pen • camera and film.

Introduction:
Tender Loving Care (TLC) is something everyone needs. As a cooperative project between home and school, consider giving some "TLC" to your classroom or school grounds. During the project, make sure that all the participants work together and receive some tender loving care in the form of refreshments, appreciation certificates, or pats on the back.

What to Do:
1. Brainstorm with staff and parents to come up with a "Tender Loving Care" project that will involve whole families. Project ideas might include washing windows, painting, re-organizing, planting a tree or garden, raking leaves, re-vitalizing a playground, building a sandbox area, or washing classroom toys and equipment.
2. If donated materials are needed, have children draw pictures of what you will need and envision the finished product. Contact local businesses to seek donations of goods or services, and include children's drawings in your requests.
3. Make one copy of the invitation on page 45. Fill in the particulars of TLC Day (date, time, project, things to bring, etc.) and then make multiple copies. Decide on a rain date, if one will be needed, or make alternate plans in case of rain.
4. Provide each child with a copy of the invitation and markers or crayons. Have children decorate the invitations and take them home.
5. On TLC Day, be sure that all supplies are readily available for your project.
6. Have jobs clearly defined, written on 3" x 5" cards. Let each person or family choose a job as they arrive. Encourage families to work as teams. Be sure to assign a "supervisor" for each job area.

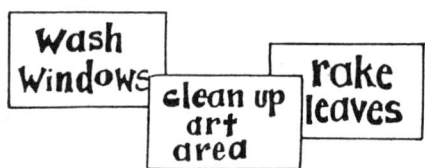

(Cards: Wash Windows / clean up art area / rake leaves)

7. Have someone take photos or videos during the day to capture "on-the-job-action"!

Challenge:
- THE COMMON GARDEN: Decide with parents, staff, and children the "who, what, where, when, and how" of your common garden. Schedule preparation, planting, and maintenance of the garden on a time line, with the classrooms, children, staff, and parents taking turns with all the jobs—including harvesting the crops.

Making Connections:
- FRIENDSHIP GARDEN: If you have no garden space around the school, consider planting on the grounds of a nursing home, in the yard of an older person (with permission and in walking distance), or in another worthy spot.

Family/School Interaction

"CELEBRATE THE FAMILY" PICNIC

CONCEPTS:
- Open communication between home and school builds family feeling.

What You'll Need:
Copies of page 45 • markers and crayons • picnic foods (prepared by families) • blankets.

Introduction:
Plan a school-family picnic or trip to a farm, a park, or a local attraction. Invite children's families to join in your "celebration of families."

What to Do:
1. Plan a picnic which focuses on the togetherness of home and school families.
2. On a copy of page 45, write the particulars of your picnic (date, time, location, rain date, etc.) Assign each family a dish to prepare for the potluck. Children whose families are not present can adopt a surrogate family for the day.
3. Make multiple copies of the invitation. Have children decorate one for their family and take it home.
4. At the picnic site, prepare a "blanket layout" (all blankets in one big circle, or in squares of four each) in order to keep the picnic organized, and to avoid families feeling "left out."
5. Plan cooperative games such as: parachute play, a song festival, field games, crafts, rope games, group charades, picnic blanket races, water balloon toss, or cooperative team challenges (see page 15 for more ideas).

Challenge:
- SCAVENGER HUNT: Make a list of items to be found. Choose items families can locate in the vicinity of the picnic area. Be sure not to make the items too difficult to locate. Prepare, copy, and distribute the scavenger hunt list to each family. Inform families when the hunt will end. Have each family bring back its completed scavenger-hunt checklist. Encourage families to add an item of their own to the scavenger list (to be used next year). Remember, everyone wins!

Making Connections:
- Teach children rhymes and have them perform during the picnic for their families. Some sources are: *Finger Rhymes, Hand Rhymes, Play Rhymes,* and *Party Rhymes*—all by Marc Brown (Dutton).

Family/School Interaction